Materials Science

D. J. Ward

LERNER PUBLICATIONS COMPANY
MINNEAPOLIS

To Nathan, who likes
to mess with matter

Text copyright © 2009 by D. J. Ward

Lerner Publications Company
A division of Lerner Publishing Group, Inc.
241 First Avenue North
Minneapolis, MN 55401 U.S.A.

Website address: www.lernerbooks.com

Library of Congress Cataloging-in-Publication Data

Ward, D. J. (David John), 1966–
        Materials science / by D. J. Ward.
            p.   cm. — (Cool science)
        Includes bibliographical references and index.
        ISBN 978–0–8225–7588–7 (lib. bdg. : alk. paper)
        1. Materials—Juvenile literature. 2. Materials science—Juvenile literature. I. Title.
    TA403.2.W37 2009
    620.1'1—dc22   2007042176

Manufactured in the United States of America
1 2 3 4 5 6 – BP – 14 13 12 11 10 09

Table of Contents

Introduction

Coming soon to a theater (or a car or a tennis racket) near you . . .

They were born in a lab. They were created with special abilities—abilities far beyond what is normal. One can bend or mold into just about any shape and can conduct electricity and heat. Another is harder than steel and can resist extreme temperatures.

Superheroes help us in extraordinary ways, and so do supermaterials.

A third is smaller than an ant, yet it has huge brainpower. The last is flexible and light but strong enough to stop a bullet.

Their mission? To totally change the future. Who are these marvels? Are they mutants? No. They are the supermaterials!

In labs around the world, scientists are learning to create new materials that have special abilities. What gives these supermaterials their powers? It's really no big thing. In fact, it's a very small thing that has to do with the tiny building blocks of all materials. The powers come from how these blocks are organized and connected at the smallest of scales.

Supermaterials start out as ordinary stuff. Scientists change the ordinary stuff in little ways. But little changes can make a big difference.

This scientist is working in a lab that looks for ways to give materials special properties.

Messing with Matter

So make a supermaterial, scientists have to mess with matter. They have to adjust it , reorganize it, and change what it's made of. But what is matter?

Matter is just a fancy word for "stuff." Whatever stuff an object is made of, it's matter. Rock is matter, for example. The air you are breathing is matter. Plants and animals are made of matter.

So what is matter made of? It is made of tiny, unbreakable pieces. Imagine that you have a cracker and you start breaking it. You keep breaking it until you can't break down the pieces anymore, no matter what you do. At this point, the cracker would just be powder. But it turns out that the cracker powder is made of smaller pieces still. These pieces are too small to see even with a microscope. They are the tiny, unbreakable building blocks that make up the cracker. These tiny pieces are called atoms. All objects everywhere are made of atoms.

How Small Is an Atom?

Earth is about 24,900 miles (40,073 kilometers) around. A tennis ball is more than 200 million times smaller—only about 8 inches (20 centimeters) around. Like everything else, tennis balls are made of atoms. Just how small are the atoms? They are as small compared to a tennis ball as a tennis ball is compared to Earth!

Since so many different types of objects are in the universe, you might think that there must be millions of kinds of atoms. Cracker atoms would make crackers, and toothpaste atoms would make toothpaste, for instance. But the whole universe has only 92 natural kinds of atoms. Many of those 92 are very rare.

IT'S A FACT!

Atoms actually can be broken down, under very unusual conditions. A nuclear explosion or a powerful machine called a nuclear accelerator can do the trick. But in everyday life, atoms are unbreakable.

Breaking down a cracker shows how all matter can become smaller and smaller down to the size of atoms.

Each kind of atom is called an element. Oxygen is a kind of atom. So are aluminum, iron, gold, silver, carbon, and tin. Helium, the gas that makes balloons float, is a kind of atom too. They're all elements. And elements are the ingredients for making everything.

So What Are Atoms Made Of?

We normally think of atoms as the building blocks of everything. But atoms are made of even tinier things: protons, neutrons, and electrons. Protons and neutrons group together to make the center of an atom, called the nucleus. Electrons form the outside of the atom. They fly around the nucleus, kind of like bees around a hive.

This is a diagram of a carbon atom. The red circles are protons. The blue circles are neutrons. Carbon has six protons and six neutrons in its nucleus. Orbiting the nucleus are six electrons.

Mix and Match

So how do you get all the billions of types of things in the universe from only 92 different ingredients? One way is to connect different kinds of atoms to one another. Each different combination makes something totally new.

For example, an element called sodium is an explosive metal when it isn't combined with other kinds of atoms. Another element called chlorine is a poisonous gas when it's by itself. But if one sodium atom is connected to one chlorine atom, it forms table salt! Yes, salt—the stuff that's stuck all over pretzels. On their own, both sodium and chlorine are dangerous to people. But together, they're edible!

Another way to make new types of matter is to change how atoms are connected. Take the element carbon. If you stick carbons together one way, you get graphite. Graphite is what makes up pencil lead. But stick carbon atoms together another way, and you get a diamond! Pure carbon can be soft enough to smear on paper or hard enough to cut steel. It all depends on how the carbon atoms are attached to one another.

The graphite in pencil lead (left) and a diamond (right) are both made of carbon. But in graphite the carbon atoms are attached to one another differently than they are in a diamond.

Think about ice cream. Ice cream comes in different flavors and colors. Some ice cream has stripes of fudge or caramel or has big chunks of stuff in it. Some kinds are light and fluffy, while others are heavy and dense.

The characteristics of ice cream—such as how it tastes, what it looks like, or how easily it scoops—are determined by things you can't see. For instance, bits of cocoa beans too small to see make chocolate ice cream brown. Its smoothness is affected by how many tiny air pockets form in the ice cream as it is made. These microscopic features of the ice cream control how it looks, tastes, and acts. The little controls the big.

The same is true for all types of materials, such as metal, plastic, glass, or wood. A material's physical properties—its hardness, its weight, and its melting temperature, for example—all are controlled by the tiniest things. These properties all depend on which elements make up the material and how the material's atoms are connected.

The Ingredients List

Check out the periodic table of the elements on page 43. The periodic table is the ingredients list for materials science. Each box stands for a different element. Different materials are created by putting together atoms from different boxes. Put together two atoms of element #1 (hydrogen) and one atom of element #8 (oxygen), and you get water—H_2O. Combine six #6s (carbon) with 12 #1s and six #8s, and you'll get sugar—$C_6H_{12}O_6$ (glucose). But if you happen to leave the oxygen out of your batch of sugar, don't taste it. It won't be food. It will be a poisonous chemical called cyclohexane! In materials science, it's important to follow the recipe.

Materials science is the study of how changing these features changes a material's physical properties. Materials scientists adjust the little stuff to change the big stuff. And those little changes make a big difference.

Around the Table

Atoms in the periodic table are arranged by how many protons they have, from least to most. The box numbers tell you how many protons each has.

Most of the atoms in the table are types of metals, such as iron (#26), gold (#79), ruthenium (#44), and hafnium (#72). The boxes on the right side are nonmetals. The elements neon (#10) and chlorine (#17) are nonmetals.

A new material can be made whenever different kinds of atoms are joined together. The possibilities are almost endless!

The Fantastic Four (Materials)

Metals, ceramics, semiconductors, and polymers. The names don't sound all that exciting. But these four types of materials are like a band of superheroes. Each has an ordinary side. You probably have some of each of them in your own bedroom. But in the hands of materials engineers, these materials each take on special abilities. They become supermaterials.

What are these materials? What makes them what they are? Let's meet them up close and personal.

Metals and Ceramics

As raw materials, metals and ceramics are nothing new. People have been making things out of them for thousands of years. But don't think that because they're old, they're past their prime. Their special abilities make metals and ceramics as useful as they've ever been.

Metals

A metal is a material made mostly of metallic elements. (Take a look at the periodic table on page 43 to see which elements are metals.) Metals can be very strong yet also flexible. They are malleable, which means they can bend without breaking. Many are good conductors of heat and electricity. Metals also are shiny. With a little polish, they can reflect as well as a mirror. Most metals are not easy to melt. They have high melting temperatures. But once melted, they can be formed into just about any shape.

Heat Thieves!

Heat travels very well through metals. You can show this in the kitchen. Put a metal spoon in the freezer. Put a wooden spoon in there too. After about 30 minutes, take out the spoons. The metal one should feel much colder.

They actually are the same temperature. After 30 minutes, they both have cooled to the temperature of the inside of the freezer. The metal spoon just feels colder because it's making *you* colder. Heat from your hand flows easily into the metal spoon but not so easily into the wooden one. The metal is stealing heat from you at a rapid rate.

At very high temperatures, metals melt (*above*). Then they can be formed into a different shape.

Why do metals have these special properties? The key to it all is what's going on with the atoms. Metal atoms just don't do things the way other atoms do.

Metal atoms don't hold very tightly onto their outer electrons. These loose electrons can drift around. They can move from one atom to another and then back again.

The ease with which some electrons move around explains a lot about metals. It explains why they can bend without breaking. It explains why electricity and heat flow through them well. It even explains why they're shiny. It's all about the electrons.

It's All about the Electrons

Why are metals good electrical conductors? Electrons are attracted (drawn in) and repelled (pushed away) by magnets and objects that have an electrical charge. Such objects make a metal's loose electrons jump from atom to atom. This flow of electrons is what we call electricity.

Why are metals good heat conductors? Temperature is all about atomic wiggling. Objects with slow-wiggling atoms feel cold. An object feels hot if its atoms are wiggling quickly. Likewise, heating something causes its atoms to wiggle faster. The loose electrons in metals are free to move and bump around like pinballs. They transfer atomic wiggling quickly throughout the metal. So if you put a metal spoon on the hot stove, it doesn't take long for the whole spoon to get hot.

Why are metals shiny? Loose electrons do a great job of reflecting light that hits a piece of metal. So the light flashes back toward our eyes and we can see it.

Alloys. On their own, many metals are not very useful. They are soft, weak, or just plain dangerous. That all changes if you mix the metals together with something else. The mixtures, called alloys, can be very useful.

Take iron, for example. On its own, iron is soft and weak—not good at all for building. But if you add a little bit of the nonmetal carbon to iron, you make an alloy called steel. Steel is perhaps the most widely used building material in the world. The carbon atoms in steel keep the iron atoms from shifting around. This makes the mixture much harder than iron alone. The more carbon that is added, the stiffer the alloy becomes. Will it be used in steel girders that need to flex without breaking during earthquakes? Add only a tiny bit of carbon. Will it

Steel girders (*left*) are used to build most large buildings (*right*). Steel is strong. It can be mixed in different ways to give the steel slightly different properties depending on its use.

become a pair of steel pliers that should grip strongly without bending? Add a little more. But if too much carbon is put in the steel, it will shatter easily when a force is applied to it.

Bronze, the first humanmade alloy, was made by melting copper with tin. Brass, the metal used to make trumpets and tubas, is copper mixed with zinc. Dinner forks, knives, and spoons are made of stainless steel, which contains iron, carbon, and chromium. The chromium atoms keep the steel shiny and rust free.

IT'S A FACT!

People have been making the alloy bronze for more than 5,000 years.

Hard or Soft?

Forces that push against one another hold atoms together. This is similar to how magnets work. The forces that hold atoms to one another are called bonds. If atoms are linked by very strong bonds, the material they make will be very strong. Weak bonds make for wimpy material.

Remember diamond and graphite? Both are pure carbon. In a diamond, the bonds are strong in every direction. So diamonds are hard in every direction. But in graphite, the carbon atoms have very strong bonds only from side to side. The bonds that connect them up and down are much weaker. Graphite is kind of like sheets of diamond with wimpy glue in between. When you write with a pencil, you're breaking the weak bonds in the graphite. You're spreading microscopic sheets of graphite across the paper with every word you write.

Ceramics

When most people hear the word *ceramic*, they usually think of clay pots or dishes. But in materials science, the term stands for much more. For instance, to a materials scientist, rubies and sapphires are ceramics. So is glass. What ceramics all have in common is that they are nonmetallic. They also aren't organic compounds. In chemistry, a material is called organic only if it is based upon combinations of carbon and hydrogen.

A ruby (*left*) and a sapphire (*right*) are both ceramics. They are neither metals nor organic compounds.

Ceramics can be even harder and stronger than metals. They don't bend much at all. Ceramics also are very heat resistant. That means they can take a lot of heat without melting. Heat doesn't pass through them easily. Ceramics generally don't conduct electricity. And unlike many metals, ceramics don't rust or corrode (break down) very easily.

Many of these properties come from the fact that, in ceramics, nothing is loose. Every atom is locked in place. No electron is allowed to roam around on its own. On the small scale—the scale of atoms—it's hard to get anything in a ceramic to change. This makes ceramics resistant to change on the big scale.

For example, corrosion is a big-scale change. For a material to corrode, atoms have to break apart from one another. But that breaking doesn't happen easily in a ceramic. So neither does corrosion.

Bend or Break?

Why do metals bend, but ceramics don't? Metal atoms are bonded as a group. When a piece of metal is bent, the connections between the atoms shift around. The atoms act kind of like a clump of ball-shaped magnets. If you pushed down on the clump, the balls would simply shift around one another. The clump would change shape but stay stuck together. This property of metals is what makes them malleable. However, it also limits metals' strength. If you apply a force to a metal, it may bend instead of holding firm.

Ceramics, on the other hand, are bonded like a cube made of Lego blocks. The bond between each atom is tight, strong, and locked in place. This is why ceramics can be stronger than steel. They can hold firm under much greater force. When they do fail, though, they break instead of bending.

Glass. Glass, one of the more common ceramics, is made mostly from ordinary beach sand. To make glass, sand is melted. If the liquid cools slowly, it will crystallize to become the mineral quartz. But if the liquid is cooled very quickly, it becomes glass.

Ordinary beach sand is made of silicon dioxide (SiO_2). If you make glass from pure SiO_2, it doesn't hold up very well. To make glass more stable, glassmakers add something called lime to the melted sand. Lime is the common name for calcium oxide (CaO). The lime keeps the glass from cracking apart. Glassmakers typically also add a substance called soda to the sand when they melt it. Soda contains sodium and oxygen (Na_2O). The soda makes the sand easier to melt. Adding these chemicals makes soda-lime glass. Soda-lime glass is by far the most common glass made in the world. It's cheap and relatively easy to make. Your windows, your drinking glass, and the jelly jar on your breakfast table probably all are soda-lime glass.

To give glass different properties, engineers change the

Most windows are made with soda-lime glass. This type of glass is cheap to make.

About 90 percent of the world's glass is made with soda and lime.

ingredients. Adding lead to glass makes it softer and more brilliant. This makes lead glass a favorite with artists who make decorative windows or glass sculptures. Adding the element boron to the mix makes glass more heat resistant. Jars used in labs are made from this type of glass. Other chemicals can be added to change the color of the glass.

Artists and glassmakers add in different chemicals to change the color of the glass they make. They can make a wide variety of colors (below).

chapter 3

Semiconductors and Polymers

If metals and ceramics are the veterans, semiconductors and human-made polymers are the rookies. These materials have been in use for fewer than 150 years. But in that short time—especially in the last few decades—they've had an amazing impact on our lives. Without them, much of the technology of modern living would not exist.

Semiconductors

Want big and tough? Think metals and ceramics. But if you need small and fast, think semiconductors. Semiconductors are famous for their brains, not for their brawn. A semiconductor is a material that does not typically conduct electricity but will if it gets enough energy. This ability allows semiconducting materials to act as tiny switches and gatekeepers in electronic equipment. They are fast and reliable. Semiconductors are the reason computers and electronic devices are smaller and smarter than ever before.

Metals often are good conductors of electricity. Nonmetals, such as ceramics, generally are not good electrical conductors. Semiconductors are in between. This is because they are made of elements that share qualities of both metals and nonmetals.

Take a look at the periodic table on page 43. Nonmetallic elements are on the far right. Metals make up the left and most of the middle. In between are a small cluster of elements whose properties are kind of like metals but also are kind of like nonmetals. For this reason, they are sometimes called the semimetals, or metalloids. This bunch includes familiar elements such as silicon (#14). Less common ones such as gallium (#31), germanium (#32), and arsenic (#33) are in there too.

Gallium (*left*) and silicon (*below*) are metalloids. They have some properties of metals and some properties of nonmetals.

The metalloids have a pretty good hold on all of their electrons. Under normal conditions, they don't let go of them. So normally, they're poor electrical conductors. But if they get hit with enough energy, electrons can get loose. The metalloids become conductors.

To illustrate, think about a bunch of people playing dodgeball. Imagine that one player is holding three balls—one in each hand and one cradled in his arms. It's hard to hold onto that many, so his grip on the one in his arms is weak. If nobody touches him, he could hold onto all three balls for the whole game. But suddenly, a ball comes flying his way! It hits the third ball in his arms. The ball pops out and rolls away, free for someone else to pick up.

Each metalloid atom is like the guy holding three dodgeballs. The balls he is holding stand for electrons. The ball flying toward him represents an outside energy source, such as sunlight or an electric charge. With a little energy boost from one of these, things get rolling. Electricity begins to flow. But without the boost, not much happens.

Super Silicon. In reality, most semiconductors are more complicated than a guy holding three dodgeballs. The most common kinds are made of two elements joined together. The different properties of each element combine to give the material its semiconducting ability.

Silicon-arsenic semiconductors work this way. They are made almost totally of silicon. Silicon's electrons usually are locked in place, unable to carry electricity. But scattered among the silicon atoms are atoms of arsenic. The arsenic has extra electrons that can roam. So when energy is added to the semiconductor, electrons get passed among the atoms.

That might not seem like a big deal. But the movement of these little

This computer chip is made with semiconducting material. This close-up picture was taken with a microscope to capture all of the detail in the tiny chip.

electrons has totally changed the way we live. Semiconductors such as these form the brains of almost every electronic device in the world. That includes cell phones, iPods, video cameras, and computers.

IT'S A FACT!

Computer chips, sometimes called silicon chips, typically are made from silicon semiconductors.

Polymers

Have you ever made a chain of paper loops? The chain can be as long as you want to make it. All you have to do is keep attaching new loops to the end. Imagine that instead of paper loops, you used loops of atoms. That's what polymers are like. They are materials made of long, chain-like molecules.

This plastic model shows the structure of a polymer chain.

Plastic is perhaps the most familiar humanmade polymer. Nature makes polymers too. (Nature made them first, of course.) Cotton, wool, and silk all are natural polymers. Cellulose, the tree fiber used to make paper, is a polymer. Most polymers are based on the element carbon. Carbon atoms are connected like a backbone down the length of the chain.

What Is a Molecule?

A molecule is a particle made from a certain combination of atoms connected together. Water, sugar, and deoxyribonucleic acid, or DNA (the chemical instructions for building a living thing), are examples of molecules. Like atoms, molecules can stay separate from one another as free-floating particles—water vapor and carbon dioxide gas, for example. Or they can act like building blocks, combining with others to make something new. This is what they do in polymers.

Polymers have an amazing range of abilities. They can be soft or hard, elastic or brittle, or slippery or sticky. They can be fluffy and delicate or tough enough to stop a bullet. They can be almost anything. One thing an ordinary polymer can't be, though, is a good conductor of electricity. In fact, polymers often are used to protect us from electricity. The plastic coating on electronic cables and cords does just that.

IT'S A FACT!

Polymers are big business. More money is spent on polymers than on steel, aluminum, and copper combined!

Make Your Own Polymer Putty

You can make your own play putty using supplies you have around the house. You need 2 cups of white school glue (Elmer's or similar), 1 cup of liquid laundry starch, and food coloring (optional).

Gradually mix the liquid starch into the glue. Use your hands to mix it in. Before too long, the glue will start to feel like a rubbery blob. Add some food coloring if you want a different color. Keep mixing in liquid starch until the blob stays together on its own, like putty. You may not need to use all the starch.

Now see what this stuff can do. You can stretch it. You can hit it. You can try to bounce it. Mash it together, and let it flow. Just don't try to dry it off—it will stick to the towel or paper you use.

How does it work? You made what is called a cross-linked polymer. The glue already is a polymer. But the chains in the glue are not connected to one another. The starch connects the glue polymer chains together. This makes it a putty instead of a runny liquid.

Plastic. Take a look at the bottom of just about any plastic container. You'll probably find a recycling symbol stamped into it. Inside the symbol, there will be a number and some letters. The letters stand for what type of material the container is made from. At least one of the letters will be the letter *P*. The *P* stands for "poly," which means "lots of." (*Poly*mer chains have lots of links.)

Most plastic containers have recycling symbols on the bottom (*left*) that tell what type of plastic was used to make the container. Not all plastics can be recycled, and these symbols help recyclers separate the different types of plastics.

Be happy that only a few letters are used, instead of the whole names. Soda pop bottles are made from polyethylene terephthalate (PETE). Milk jugs often are high-density polyethylene (HDPE). Yogurt comes in polypropylene (PP) containers.

Actually, the names are not hard to understand. After *poly* ("lots of"), the rest of the word tells what there are lots of. Polypropylene is made from lots of propylene molecules connected together. Propylene makes up the links of the big, long polymer chain in yogurt containers.

Different plastics are used to package different foods. Manufacturers use the polymer that will best meet the needs of the product. For instance, some foods are put into their containers hot at the factory. Other foods need to be microwaved. Those foods aren't put in polyethylene, which

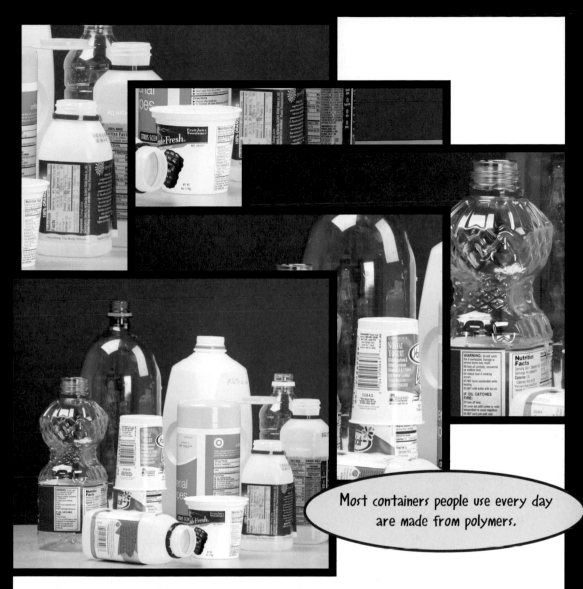

Most containers people use every day are made from polymers.

will warp or melt if it gets very hot. Polypropylene is a much better choice for hot jobs. But polyethylene is great for soda pop, which is cold from start to finish.

Plastics come in two main types: thermoplastics and thermosets. Thermoplastics can be melted and reused. All the plastic things you find that have the recycling symbol on them are thermoplastics. Thermosets cannot be recycled. This is because they don't melt when heated—they just burn. So a thermoset object can't be formed into something else.

What's the difference? In a thermoplastic, the polymer chains are not connected very tightly to one another. A thermoplastic is kind of like a pile of unlinked metal chains. You can easily separate one chain from another one. This is what happens when a thermoplastic is melted. The chains separate from one another and make a liquid.

Yes, Your Toothbrush Is Made from Oil

Most humanmade polymers are made from fossil fuels such as oil. We normally think of oil as an energy source. But it also holds the building blocks of plastics.

The chemicals used as raw materials for making plastics are separated out of the oil. This happens at oil refineries. Refineries then ship these chemicals to plastics companies. At the plastics plant, the raw materials are combined with other chemicals to make different materials. They may make polymers such as nylon, used in toothbrush bristles, or polypropylene, used to make toothbrush handles. Thousands of plastic products around the house started as oil.

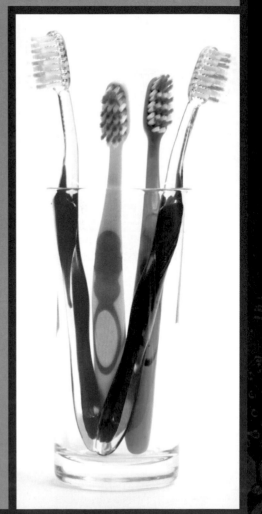

Toothbrushes and other plastic items are made from the same source as gasoline.

This engineer is holding shredded plastic waste (*left*) and the liquid it is melted into so it can be reused.

In a thermoset, the polymer chains bond together tightly. It's more like a chain-link fence than a box of loose chains. The chains stay connected even at high temperatures. This makes thermosets useful for things you don't want to break down, such as automobile and boat parts, furniture, toys, and even high-strength glue.

Because polymers can be used in so many ways, they have become more common than traditional materials, such as metal and wood, in everyday objects. Right now, you're probably holding one, wearing one, or sitting on one. These days, you're never very far from a polymer.

chapter 4

Supermaterials in Action

We don't have to wait for a crime or a natural disaster for the supermaterials to swing into action. They already are at work all around us. And their special abilities are changing the way we live.

Lessons from a Snail

Sometimes the best way to develop new supermaterials is to get ideas from nature. Plants and animals already create some amazing materials, from which we can learn.

The red abalone, a sea snail, needs a hard shell to protect itself from animals that would eat it. Instead of making its shell from one thick material, the snail builds its shell in layers. It alternates layers of hard limestone with layers of flexible protein. Each layer is very thin—less than one thousandth the thickness of a human hair! But this process makes the abalone's shell very tough for its thickness.

This red abalone shell looks different on the inside (*left*) and outside because of its many layers.

Researchers at the University of California at San Diego have matched the abalone's technique. Using foil-thin layers of titanium alloy and a ceramic-like material, they created a supertough shell of their own. A piece of the material 0.75 inch (2 cm) thick was able to stop a heavy, metal object flying 2,000 miles per hour (3,219 kilometers per hour)!

IT'S A FACT!

Piezoelectric materials—things that give off an electric shock when squeezed—are used to release air bags in cars.

Scientists think materials such as this could be useful one day as military armor. Electronics could be built into the layers to give the material the ability to send signals when it is damaged. Of course, nature already makes a protective material that can sense when it's damaged. It's called skin. So when it comes to both strength and sensitivity, nature's a great role model.

Bullet-Stopping Plastic

Modern bulletproof vests are made of polyethylene, a polymer. That's the same stuff most milk jugs are made from. But the material used in vests is a different kind of polyethylene. It's called ultra-high molecular weight polyethylene (UHMWPE). UHMWPE is up to 30 times denser than milk jug plastic. UHMWPE is 10 times stronger than steel, yet is light enough to float on water. Fibers of UHMWPE are woven together into a superstrong but flexible mesh. Inside a vest, this mesh becomes a lifesaver.

If You Can't Stand the Heat, Get Out of the Jet Engine

Jet engines run hot—very hot. Inside a jet engine is a turbine. A turbine is kind of like a high-tech pinwheel. In making a jet engine turbine, not just any metal will do. It needs metal that can stand up to blasts of superheated gases while spinning more than 10,000 times per minute. And it needs to be able to keep doing that hour after hour and day after day, with no breaks. Talk about high stress!

Jet engine turbine blades are made from superalloys. These super metals are made mostly of nickel. Superalloys can stand up to high temperatures for long periods without weakening.

But even super metals can have weak spots. This would be a problem in a turbine blade. Any weakness would cause the blade to break at that

Turbine blades for jet engines (*above*) are made from superalloys so they can stand up to extreme temperatures.

spot while in use. To prevent this, each turbine blade is one big crystal of metal. Here's how it works. If not poured in a mold, molten metal cools and hardens in patches that spread outward. Each of these patches is a metal crystal. Where the crystals meet, the metal is weaker than in the centers of the crystals. Turbine blades are carefully molded and cooled to have no such weak spots.

IT'S A FACT!

Ceramic tiles made of glass protect space shuttles from the high heat of reentering Earth's atmosphere.

Superalloys are strong under fire. So why don't we use them for all kinds of things? Because they're expensive. Cheaper metals work just fine for most things. But jet engine turbine blades are worth the cost. If one broke while an airplane was flying, hundreds of lives could be lost.

Keeping It Cool

Refrigerators and freezers are wonderful. However, they have a downside. They use chemicals called hydrofluorocarbons (HFCs) to cool the air inside. HFCs are greenhouse gases. When released, these gases add to the problem of global warming.

Some scientists with the U.S. Department of Energy think they have a pollution-free solution: magnetic refrigeration. Materials called magnetocalorics change temperature when exposed to magnetic fields. Refrigerators could be made with magnetocaloric materials inside. Plugging in your refrigerator would turn on magnets. The magnets would make the magnetocaloric materials cold, chilling the food inside as well. The result? Cold leftovers without the pollution.

Hovercars?

In general, ceramics can't conduct electricity. In fact, sometimes they are used to protect people from getting shocked. But certain kinds of ceramics have a hidden talent. When they get really cold, they transform into superconductors. Superconductors are perfect transmitters of electricity. They can do it without building up any heat or losing any energy. They also can completely repel magnets. No one really knows how these amped-up ceramics work. But scientists are excited about what they can do.

Imagine driving around town in a floating car. Superconductors may make that a reality by using something called magnetic levitation (mag-lev). Maglev vehicles ride atop magnetic fields. Magnets in the road repel magnets in the vehicle, making the vehicle hover. Since superconductors repel magnets better than anything, they are the perfect levitators. Maglev trains on magnetic rails already are up and running in some countries. These trains are quiet, smooth, and really fast. One Japanese maglev train can travel nearly 400 mph (644 kph)!

SMT

Top: This ceramic disc is floating by magnetic levitation. *Bottom:* The Shanghai Transrapid train in China uses magnetic levitation.

Superconducting ceramics would already be everywhere if it weren't for one thing. They need to be downright frigid to work. They have to be chilled to at least −211°F (−135°C) or they won't superconduct. But scientists are working on making materials that will do the trick at warmer temperatures. And when they figure it out, everyone's going to get a lift.

Faster, Higher, Stronger

In sports, the difference between winning and losing often is a tiny margin. It may be an inch (2.5 cm) here or a fraction of a second there. As a result, athletes look for any edge they can get. Using athletic equipment made from supermaterials can give them the extra boost they're looking for.

One such material is a composite (a material made from combinations of material types). Carbon fiber composite has totally changed sporting equipment. It uses threadlike carbon fibers made of twisted-up sheets of graphite. Each fiber of carbon is thinner than a human hair. But these fibers are incredibly strong for their size and weight. Plus, they're flexible. In carbon fiber composite material, the fibers are covered in plastic polymer. The result is a material that is tough, strong, flexible, and light.

Go to any sporting goods store, and carbon fiber composite will be all around you. It's used to make high-performance bike frames and rims. It's molded into helmets for biking, snowboarding, skateboarding, and kayaking. Carbon fiber clubs help golfers drive the ball hundreds of feet farther than they could 30 years ago. Many tennis rackets are made from carbon fiber composite. It's even used to make fishing rods. Look out, fish!

Getting an edge in sports with supermaterials seems like a winning idea. But some people think using materials like these gives athletes an unfair advantage. Sports should be about the athlete, not the gear, they say. Some sports organizations have outlawed the use of certain high-tech equipment. They hope to keep the game in the hands of the players and out of the hands of engineers.

Nanotubular!

Bonded one way, pure carbon makes graphite. Bonded another way, it makes diamond. But carbon has yet another ability. It can be formed into nanotubes.

Nano means "very, very small." Carbon nanotubes are about 100,000 times thinner than a human hair! These tiny tubes of carbon have some amazing properties. They are great conductors of both heat and electricity. (Neither graphite nor diamond can claim this.) And carbon nanotubes are flexible, yet incredibly strong—up to 100 times stronger than steel!

Carbon nanotubes already have been mixed into metal alloys,

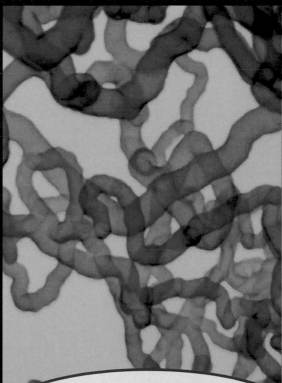

This photograph, taken with an electron microscope, shows carbon nanotubes.

such as steel. This strength-
ens the alloy without adding weight. Because of this
advantage, nanotubes are

in high-tech bike frames, baseball bats, and other
sports equipment.

Scientists also have figured out how to arrange carbon nanotubes into shapes. This may make it possible
to build objects out of them.

One of these objects could be artificial muscle for
people. Muscles work by receiving electrical signals
from the brain. And they must be able to take a lot of
stress and still flex back into shape. Since nanotubes
are good electrical conductors, they might be able
to receive brain signals. Also, their combination of
strength and flexibility may make them perfect for
the job.

Attached like hairs to a plastic polymer strip, carbon
nanotubes make gecko tape. This tape can repeat-
edly stick to walls and unstick just like geckos' feet. In fact, nanotube
tape actually has a stronger grip. Imagine wall-climbing robots with
nanotube gecko feet! Nanotube tape may also come in handy in space.
The lack of air in space makes regular tape less sticky. But nanotube tape
would hold its grip.

One day, carbon nanotubes may also be used like tiny wires. Scientists
think nanotube wires will be up to six times lighter than traditional copper wire and up to ten times better at conducting electricity. This will

allow electronic devices to become smaller, lighter, and faster. Astronauts are interested in nanotube wires too. Replacing copper wires with nanotubes will make spacecraft lighter, requiring less fuel.

The day of the nanotube wire may be coming soon. Already, researchers have made a working computer chip using nanotube wires. The tube is definitely the shape of things to come.

Be Like a Leaf

People are just learning how to harvest solar energy. Plants, however, have always known how. So plants serve as a good model for people to study.

Traditional, humanmade solar cells use silicon semiconductor crystals to turn solar energy into electricity. Plants harvest light energy using polymers. Researchers are studying how plants do this. The goal is to match their process. Scientists have already made polymer-based solar cells that are lighter, more flexible, and less expensive than traditional silicon kinds.

Solar panels are used to harvest energy from sunlight.

Some problems of these new solar cells still need to be solved. The main problem is that polymer solar cells don't create electricity quite as well as silicon-based ones. But scientists are working on them. Solar cells modeled after leaves may be right around the corner.

A Bright Idea

What if your computer worked at the speed of light? That time may be here in a flash.

Computers operate by sending electrical signals between their parts. Tomorrow's computers may use light. Engineers are working on computer parts made of see-through polymers and ultrapure glass. Light-based computers will be faster than today's computers. They will be smaller. They won't get hot, either. The future for computing looks bright.

Metal with a Memory

Fold your fingers into your hand. Now let go. Your hand will naturally open back up. When your brain isn't sending the signal to grip, your hand's muscles relax to their normal positions. They seem to remember how they were before you moved them.

Materials scientists have found metal alloys that can do almost the same thing. They're called shape memory alloys (SMAs). When cool, SMAs are easy to bend and mold. But if you bend one and then heat it up, it will flex back to its original shape. And if you put enough pressure on a hot SMA to bend it and then let go, it will unbend.

SMAs already have been used to make tiny, flexible surgical tools such as clamps and twee-zers. These tools can be inserted into the body through a small hole and then heated to change shape. Orthodontists are using SMA wires in braces. SMA wires pull more gen-tly than traditional stain-less steel wires, causing less mouth pain.

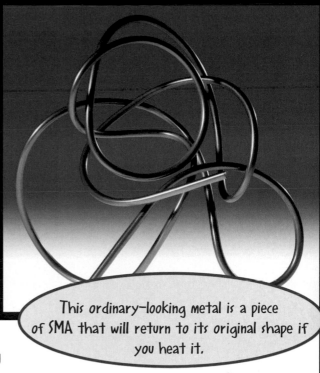

This ordinary-looking metal is a piece of SMA that will return to its original shape if you heat it.

Scientists think SMAs could also be useful for controlling the movements of things like airplane flaps. They may even be used one day to create artificial muscles for robots and robotic artificial limbs for people.

Future Trends

What does the future hold for supermaterials? In the future, super-materials will not work alone. More and more, they will join forces. Composites are on the rise. Engineers are combining metals with ce-ramics, ceramics with polymers, and polymers with metals. Composites boast the best properties of each material.

In the future, materials will be "intelligent." Engineers are working on materials that can respond instantly to changes in their environment. Imagine metals that can sense when they are corroding and put a stop to it. Picture plastics that can heal themselves when they break. Tomorrow's materials will be able to react.

In the future, materials will create more medical miracles. A new class of supermaterials called biomaterials is in the works. They are designed to act like living tissue. One day soon, patients with severe burns will be healed using humanmade skin. Artificial bone will fuse together with natural bone in the limbs of amputees. Using biomaterials, doctors will be able to save and improve more lives.

Materials of the future will be better than older ones. They will be stronger, lighter, tougher, faster, and safer. Like modern supermaterials, tomorrow's materials will start out as ordinary stuff. Scientists will change the ordinary stuff in little ways. And those little changes will make a big difference in our lives.

Periodic Table of the Elements

Legend:
- metals
- metalloids
- nonmetals

1	2	3	4	5	6	7	8	9	10	11	12	13	14	15	16	17	18
H HYDROGEN 1																	He HELIUM 2
Li LITHIUM 3	Be BERYLLIUM 4											B BORON 5	C CARBON 6	N NITROGEN 7	O OXYGEN 8	F FLUORINE 9	Ne NEON 10
Na SODIUM 11	Mg MAGNESIUM 12											Al ALUMINUM 13	Si SILICON 14	P PHOSPHORUS 15	S SULFUR 16	Cl CHLORINE 17	Ar ARGON 18
K POTASSIUM 19	Ca CALCIUM 20	Sc SCANDIUM 21	Ti TITANIUM 22	V VANADIUM 23	Cr CHROMIUM 24	Mn MANGANESE 25	Fe IRON 26	Co COBALT 27	Ni NICKEL 28	Cu COPPER 29	Zn ZINC 30	Ga GALLIUM 31	Ge GERMANIUM 32	As ARSENIC 33	Se SELENIUM 34	Br BROMINE 35	Kr KRYPTON 36
Rb RUBIDIUM 37	Sr STRONTIUM 38	Y YTTRIUM 39	Zr ZIRCONIUM 40	Nb NIOBIUM 41	Mo MOLYBDENUM 42	Tc TECHNETIUM 43	Ru RUTHENIUM 44	Rh RHODIUM 45	Pd PALLADIUM 46	Ag SILVER 47	Cd CADMIUM 48	In INDIUM 49	Sn TIN 50	Sb ANTIMONY 51	Te TELLURIUM 52	I IODINE 53	Xe XENON 54
Cs CESIUM 55	Ba BARIUM 56	La-Lu LANTHANIDES 57-71	Hf HAFNIUM 72	Ta TANTALUM 73	W TUNGSTEN 74	Re RHENIUM 75	Os OSMIUM 76	Ir IRIDIUM 77	Pt PLATINUM 78	Au GOLD 79	Hg MERCURY 80	Tl THALLIUM 81	Pb LEAD 82	Bi BISMUTH 83	Po POLONIUM 84	At ASTATINE 85	Rn RADON 86
Fr FRANCIUM 87	Ra RADIUM 88	Ac-Lr ACTINIDES 89-103	Rf RUTHERFORDIUM 104	Db DUBNIUM 105	Sg SEABORGIUM 24	Bh BOHRIUM 107	Hs HASSIUM 108	Mt MEITNERIUM 109	Ds DARMSTADTIUM 110	Rg ROENTGENIUM 111							

lanthanides

La LANTHANUM 57	Ce CERIUM 58	Pr PRASEODYMIUM 59	Nd NEODYMIUM 60	Pm PROMETHIUM 61	Sm SAMARIUM 62	Eu EUROPIUM 63	Gd GADOLINIUM 64	Tb TERBIUM 65	Dy DYSPROSIUM 66	Ho HOLMIUM 67	Er ERBIUM 68	Tm THULIUM 69	Yb YTTERBIUM 70	Lu LUTETIUM 71

actinides

Ac ACTINIUM 89	Th THORIUM 90	Pa PROTACTINIUM 91	U URANIUM 92	Np NEPTUNIUM 93	Pu PLUTONIUM 94	Am AMERICIUM 95	Cm CURIUM 96	Bk BERKELIUM 97	Cf CALIFORNIUM 98	Es EINSTEINIUM 99	Fm FERMIUM 100	Md MENDELEVIUM 101	No NOBELIUM 102	Lr LAWRENCIUM 103

Glossary

alloy: a substance made of a blend of different metals or of a metal and a nonmetal. The blend gives the alloy special properties that a pure metal would not have on its own.

bond: a force holding atoms or molecules together

ceramic: any nonmetallic, heat-resistant material that is not based on carbon and hydrogen

composite: a material made from a combination of other material types, such as metal and polymer or polymer and ceramic

compound: a molecule made from multiple types of atoms (elements)

corrode: to break down by slowly changing into a new substance because of a chemical reaction. Rust on steel is an example of corrosion.

element: a type of atom

materials science: the study of how changing the ingredients or atomic structure of a material changes its physical properties

metal: a material made mostly of metallic elements

metalloid: an element that has characteristics of both metals and nonmetals

molecule: a particle made of a combination of atoms

organic compound: a material made from combinations of carbon and hydrogen atoms. Most of your body is made from organic compounds.

periodic table of the elements: a chart that lists the elements in order by number of protons. The periodic table also gives the elements' masses and other properties.

polymer: a material composed of long, chainlike molecules. Molecules in polymers usually are carbon based.

semiconductor: a material that does not typically conduct electricity but will if enough energy hits it

superconductor: a perfect conductor of electricity. Superconductors transmit electricity without losing energy or making heat.

Selected Bibliography

BCIT. "Chem 0010: Introductory Applied Chemistry." *Chemistry Department, British Columbia Institute of Technology*. 2006. http://nobel.scas.bcit.ca/chem0010/ (April 30, 2008).

Case Western Reserve University. "Introduction to Polymers." *PLC*. 2004. http://plc .cwru.edu/tutorial/enhanced/files/polymers/intro.htm (April 30, 2008).

GlassOnWeb. 2008. http://www.glassonweb.com/ (April 29, 2008).

Goo, Edward. "Ceramics." *University of Southern California*. N.d. http://www-classes .usc.edu/engr/ms/125/MDA125/ceramics_files/frame.htm (April 29, 2008).

———"Metals." *University of Southern California*. N.d. http://www-classes.usc.edu/ engr/ms/125/MDA125/metals_files/frame.htm (April 30, 2008).

———"Polymers." *University of Southern California*. N.d. http://www-classes.usc.edu/ engr/ms/125/MDA125/polymers_files/frame.htm (April 30, 2008).

National Academy of Sciences. *The Physics of Materials: How Science Improves Our Lives*. Washington, DC: National Academy Press, 1997.

New Materials International. 2008. http://www.newmaterials.com/ (April 30, 2008).

ScienceDaily. 2008. http://www.sciencedaily.com/ (April 30, 2008).

"Superalloys." The Superalloy Committee of the Specialty Steel Industry of North America. N.d. http://www.ussuperalloys.com/ (April 30, 2008).

University of Illinois. "Materials Science and Technology Teacher's Workshop." *Department of Materials Science and Engineering, University of Illinois–Urbana-Champaign*. N.d. http://matse1.mse.uiuc.edu/ (April 30, 2008).

University of Michigan. "Materials Science and Engineering." *University of Michigan*. 2005. http://www.mse.engin.umich.edu/ (April 30, 2008).

Wilbraham, Antony C., ed. *Prentice Hall Chemistry*. Upper Saddle River, NJ: Pearson Prentice Hall, 2004.

Winter, Mark. "WebElements: The Periodic Table on the Web." *University of Sheffield and WebElements*. 2007. http://www.webelements.com/webelements/scholar/ (April 30, 2008).

Callister, William D., Jr. *Materials Science and Engineering: An Introduction,* 7th ed. New York: John Wiley & Sons, 2007.

Eberhart, Mark. *Why Things Break: Understanding the World by the Way It Comes Apart.* New York: Harmony Books, 2003.

Firestone, Mary. *Wireless Technology.* Minneapolis: Lerner Publications Company, 2009.

Fridell, Ron. *Sports Technology.* Minneapolis: Lerner Publications Company, 2009.

Gordon, J. E. *The New Science of Strong Materials or Why You Don't Fall through the Floor.* Princeton, NJ: Princeton University Press, 2006.

How Stuff Works
http://www.howstuffworks.com/
This website contains information on a wide variety of topics, including science and technology. Search the site to find out more about atoms, electricity, nanotubes, and much more.

Johnson, Rebecca L. *Nanotechnology.* Minneapolis: Lerner Publications Company, 2006.

Kerrod, Robin. *New Materials.* Mankato, MN: Smart Apple Media, 2004.

Miller, Jeanne. *Food Science.* Minneapolis: Lerner Publications Company, 2009.

The Polymer Science Learning Center
http://www.pslc.ws/
This site is filled with polymer information and activities for students.

WebElements: The Periodic Table on the Web
http://www.webelements.com/webelements/scholar/
This page features an interactive period table with links to information about all of the elements.

Woodford, Chris, Ben Morgan, and Clint Witchalls. *Cool Stuff and How It Works.* New York: DK Publishing, 2005.

Index

Photo Acknowledgments

The images in this book are used with the permission of: © Fotolia.com/AGphotographer, pp. 1, 2, 4, 6, 8, 10, 12, 14, 16, 18, 20, 22, 24, 26, 28, 30, 32, 34, 36, 38, 40, 42, 44, 46, (background); © iStockphoto.com/ AdiniMalibuBarbie, p. 4; © U. Bellhaeuser/ScienceFoto/Getty Images, p. 5; © Todd Strand/Independent Picture Service, pp. 7, 9 (right), 26, 27; © Bill Hauser/Independent Picture Service, pp. 8, 43; © Steve Lewis/ Photographer's Choice/Getty Images, p. 9 (left); © Brand X Pictures, p. 13; © Photodisc/Getty Images, p. 15 (left); © Stuart McCall/Stone/Getty Images, p. 15 (right); ©Taro Kumamoto/Photonica/Getty Images, p. 16; © John Kreul/Independent Picture Service, p. 18; © A.A.M. Van der Heyden/Independent Picture Service, p. 19; (C) Yoav Levy/ PHOTOTAKE, p. 21(left); © Peter Ginter/Science Faction/Getty Images, p. 21(right); © H.U. Danzebrink/ScienceFoto/Getty Images, p. 23; © Leslie Garland Picture Library/Alamy, p. 24; © iStockphoto. com/Jonathan Maddock, p. 28; © James-King Holmes/Photo Researchers, Inc., p. 29; © Matthew Ward/ Dorling Kindersley/Getty Images, p. 31; © iStockphoto.com/Serghei Starus , p. 33; © Takeshi Takahara/Photo Researchers, Inc., p. 35(top); ©Jay M. Pasachoff/Science Faction/Getty Images, p. 35 (bottom); © Dennis Kunkel/PHOTOTAKE, Inc./Alamy, p. 37; © Getty Images, p. 38; © Lester Lefkowitz/Stone/Getty Images, p. 39; © Phil Degginger/Alamy, p. 41.

Front Cover: © iStockphoto.com/John Clines, (top left); © Scott Camazine/Alamy (center); © iStockphoto.com/ Christian Lagereek, (bottom right); © Fotolia.com/AGphotographer (background).

About the Author

David Ward lives in Elizabeth, Colorado, with his wife and two sons. He teaches high school physics, geology, and astronomy. Ward is active in his local church and enjoys hiking with his family. He also enjoys bicycling, playing basketball, and playing bass guitar (but never at the same time).